AN IDEAS INTO ACTION GUIDEBOOK

Selling Your Ideas to Your Organization

IDEAS INTO ACTION GUIDEBOOKS

Aimed at managers and executives who are concerned with their own and others' development, each guidebook in this series gives specific advice on how to complete a developmental task or solve a leadership problem.

LEAD CONTRIBUTOR	Harold Scharlatt
CONTRIBUTORS	Craig Chappelow
	Gene Klann
	Don Prince
	Stephanie Trovas
	Drew Whitler
DIRECTOR OF PUBLICATIONS	Martin Wilcox
EDITOR AND WRITER	Peter Scisco
ASSOCIATE EDITOR	Karen Lewis
DESIGN AND LAYOUT	Joanne Ferguson
CONTRIBUTING ARTISTS	Laura J. Gibson
	Chris Wilson, 29 & Company

CCL No. 439
ISBN No. 978-1-60491-025-4

CENTER FOR CREATIVE LEADERSHIP
POST OFFICE BOX 26300
GREENSBORO, NORTH CAROLINA 27438-6300
336-288-7210
WWW.CCL.ORG / PUBLICATIONS

AN IDEAS INTO ACTION GUIDEBOOK

Selling Your Ideas to Your Organization

Harold Scharlatt

Center for
Creative
Leadership

NORTH AMERICA EUROPE ASIA

www.ccl.org

THE IDEAS INTO ACTION GUIDEBOOK SERIES

This series of guidebooks draws on the practical knowledge that the Center for Creative Leadership (CCL®) has generated, since its inception in 1970, through its research and educational activity conducted in partnership with hundreds of thousands of managers and executives. Much of this knowledge is shared—in a way that is distinct from the typical university department, professional association, or consultancy. CCL is not simply a collection of individual experts, although the individual credentials of its staff are impressive; rather it is a community, with its members holding certain principles in common and working together to understand and generate practical responses to today's leadership and organizational challenges.

The purpose of the series is to provide managers with specific advice on how to complete a developmental task or solve a leadership challenge. In doing that, the series carries out CCL's mission to advance the understanding, practice, and development of leadership for the benefit of society worldwide. We think you will find the Ideas Into Action Guidebooks an important addition to your leadership toolkit.

Table of Contents

EXECUTIVE BRIEF

When you want to sell an idea to your organization, there are two important things to consider: an environmental scan and a collection of tactics. This guidebook explains how to assess your environment, point by point. It also provides a collection of tactics you can use to sell your idea. Assessing your environment and considering tactics you can use will prepare you for a successful campaign, and you will be more likely to accomplish your objective—solving a problem or making an improvement for the benefit of individuals, groups, and the organization as a whole.

After the Brainstorm

You've got an idea that you want to sell to your organization. Maybe it's a project that you want to be in charge of. Or maybe it's a piece of a bigger project that you want to move forward. It could be an improvement on an existing process or just something that you believe will make your group, team, or organization function better. You want others to understand and endorse your

idea, to line up in support of it before you take it public and risk a false start.

If you don't have a strategy for selling your idea, you face several risks. You may not be able to accomplish your objective: the problem may not be solved or the improvement may not be made. Others may perceive you as ineffective and unable to follow through. Your direct reports may lose confidence in you. And if *you* don't sell your idea and accomplish your objective, your competitor might. Ouch!

If you want to be successful in getting others to consider and adopt your ideas, there are two important things to consider. First is an environmental scan. A scan of your organization clarifies your situation in relation to the people you have to influence as part of selling your ideas. The second element is a collection of tactics that you can employ when you begin trying to sell your ideas. This guidebook examines both of those components.

Scanning Your Organization

By assessing your organizational environment, you lay the groundwork for success in getting your ideas accepted and implemented. The several points that follow can provide you with the information you need to get started. It is not essential to assess the points in this order, but this is a logical sequence, in that one thing tends to build on another. Assessing these points will tell you what you know—and don't know. If you attempt to assess one of the points and don't come up with an answer, that's important. You will have to decide whether to proceed with a gap in your knowledge or to try harder to get an answer.

The Fit with Your Organization's Goals

Your organization's explicit goals are recorded (and, ideally, well communicated). You can find evidence of them in its vision statement, its mission, its strategic objectives, its structure, and other forms. On the other hand, the implicit goals of your organization are less visible. These are the "what we try to do around here" ideas that people carry with them, believe, and act on. The more closely you can align your ideas with your organization's spoken and unspoken goals, the better chance you have of getting your ideas accepted and implemented.

For example, let's assume that your organization places a high value on teamwork across its divisions. That's a goal it states in its working principles, and it's a practice that managers throughout the organization strive to achieve. If you tie your idea to a sense of teamwork, if you can present it as supporting and enabling that particular goal, there's a good chance that people will support it. The opposite also holds true. If your idea goes against any of your organization's written goals, objectives, or values—or the unwritten ones—or if it goes against the grain of common practice, it will be very difficult, if not impossible, for you to get support for your idea, no matter how beneficial it may be. You're going to have to make a much more difficult push to get your idea sold, and you have to plan for that accordingly. People have to see the benefit right away, and one way to help them see that is to align your ideas with what they want to achieve.

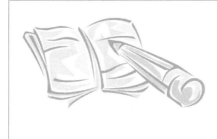

Leadership Task
Gather your organization's mission statement, vision statement, and strategic plan. What are the explicit goals suggested in those documents?

Your Group's (and Your Own) Position in Your Organization

Make a frank assessment of your group's position (and your personal position) in the true hierarchy of your organization. To make this assessment, you'll need to go beyond the official organizational chart and become aware of the unwritten pecking order—the informal power structure, which is often very different from the organizational chart. That order can change with different circumstances, such as increased competition, a new CEO, or some other realignment. Consider your organization. Does the sales force drive your organization's work, or is it the finance group or the marketing group? Is production the driving force, or does your organization measure itself in the number of grants it receives? What about innovation, research, and development? Do those functions create the heart of your organization? Whatever your answer, how are you positioned in relation to the driving forces in your organization? Are you part of them, or do you work outside of those functions? These are the kinds of relationships that determine the true hierarchy of your organization.

For example, if you're a group director in the manufacturing end of your organization, and you've got an idea for improving a production process, you may realize that you need support from the finance group in order to procure the new equipment that your improvement requires. You know also that financials drive many of your organization's decisions. In the true hierarchy, even though you have the same title as a group director in finance, you are really not at the same level. This is the kind of relationship you need to assess and consider. You want to determine where you and your group are positioned in the structure that reflects how things work in your organization.

Leadership Task

Get a copy of the organizational chart. Then draw your own chart, but instead of reporting relationships, think of the informal power structure in your organization. How do things get done? Represent more powerful groups with larger blocks or circles. Draw arrows that represent how ideas and projects move through the organization—for example, does everything need to pass through finance? Does your idea need buy-in from IT? See the example on page 11.

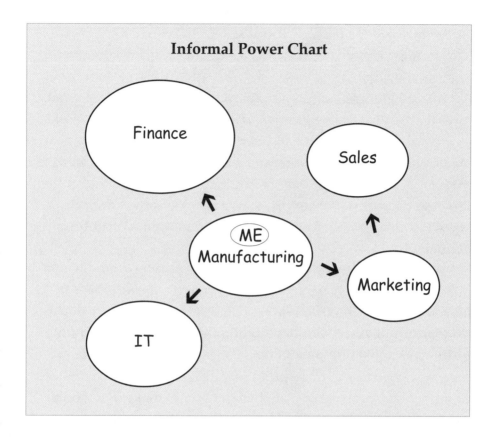

Become aware of the unwritten pecking order—the informal power structure, which is often very different from the organizational chart.

Support Needed from Key People in Key Groups

Among the groups that you've identified as important in your organization's true hierarchy, there are people who must at some level endorse your ideas. You will need to determine what level that is. From some group leaders you will only need an okay or a mutual understanding of your ideas. From some other group leaders you may need a willingness to help, and you may want to measure to what degree they can be helpful and what kind of help they can provide. For example, you may want some groups to share resources, while from others you need communication support.

To increase your chances of success in getting your ideas adopted, it's important that you make your needs very clear to each crucial group. What's more, you need to make your solicitation for support and your expectation for a level of support especially clear to the leaders in these groups. If you need official approval from any of these groups or their leaders, you may need to make a more formal appeal than you might make if you only need a group's tacit approval.

Leadership Task

List the groups you need to work with to get your idea sold, identify the key people in those groups, and describe the level of support you need from them.

Levels of Support for Your Idea

I'll do it!

I'll work with you.

I'll supply resources.

I'll actively support it.

I'll give you advice.

It's okay.

I'm neutral.

I won't sabotage it.

Resources

Just about any new idea requires resources to implement. The resource you need may be money, but just as often you need staff, equipment, access to data, access to expertise, administrative support, storage, and other noncash resources. You may not be able to describe the resources you need by a monetary amount, but they still have to be accounted for. Organizations typically align resources toward achieving their goals, and accommodating a new idea may require shifting that alignment.

Also keep in mind the competition for resources inside your organization. In considering the resources you need for selling and implementing your idea, who or what other group is competing for the same resources? Compare your idea with their work. Think about how to integrate or match up the two so that resources can be shared for mutual benefit.

Integration and sharing may not be possible. In that case, you should analyze your likely adversaries in competing for resources. You should also take stock of your likely allies—those people and groups you've identified as possible supporters.

Leadership Task

List the groups or people who have resources you need. Think about how you can request those resources in the context of other people's making the same request. Who will likely be pushing back against your idea for whatever reasons? Try to think about their reasons from their perspective. And who are your likely allies?

Allies, Adversaries . . . and More Adversaries

You will have allies and adversaries, and there will be a third group as well—those who just want to maintain the status quo. There are some people who just like for things to stay the way they are. Even though they may not be competing for the resources you need, they'd rather not get involved with your idea. It may create too much work for them, it may change their power base, or it may cause them to do things they're not too comfortable with. They are people who, for one reason or another, just don't want to be bothered. They wind up being adversaries—maybe not as strong, but certainly in that group.

Depending on your organization, this group could be a large percentage. The environmental scan will help determine how open your organization is to change.

Your Group's Commitment to Your Idea

It's obvious and therefore easy to overlook, but before you try to sell a new idea to other parts of your organization, make sure that people in your own group support it. Otherwise, somebody in your group could sabotage your idea with a simple remark in the hall. For example, someone outside Mary's group approaches and says to one of her group members, "I was just talking to Mary about her idea." And Mary's group member replies, "Well, I'm not crazy about it. It's all Mary's idea, and I don't think it'll fly." If the people in your own group don't fully support your idea, your chances of garnering external support are dramatically reduced.

Sabotage can be unintentional. Let's say, for example, that a group leader from another part of your organization is riding the elevator with one of your group members and mentions that he has heard something about a new idea you've brought up. Your group member says, "I don't know much about it. He's always coming up with new ideas." The other group leader is likely to feel that he doesn't need to put any energy into supporting it if your own group members don't even know much about it.

Intentional or not, these missteps can be avoided if you ask for input and get your group's support before going out to talk to other people about your idea. Keep in mind that the number of people in your group could be larger than you think—larger, say, than the people who report directly to you. People outside your group may perceive that more people are aligned with your group than what's on the organizational chart (the true hierarchy revealing itself).

Before you try to sell a new idea to other parts of your organization, make sure that people in your own group support it.

Those Who May Feel Threatened

Despite all the discussion about flatter structures with more permeable internal boundaries, there is still territorial conflict in organizations. When you introduce an idea, some groups or individuals may feel that you're treading on their turf and become defensive. That creates an obstacle to getting your idea accepted and implemented.

For example, if you're the leader of a product group with an idea for marketing a product, and you introduce the idea to the marketing group leader, she may agree that it's a great idea. "But that's really our job," she says. "Oh, good," you say. "So you're going to work on it?" And she replies, "No, we're not going to work on that. We've got other priorities just now." So then you say, "I understand. I think my group can get to work on it." At that point she says, "No, it's our job. It's really our responsibility." She is asking you not to implement the idea because it's her group's responsibility, yet she is not willing to have her group take action. She feels that you're treading on her group's territory, and she is defending that territory.

Others Who Can Help Sell or Implement Your Idea

At an early stage, run your idea by people to see if you can get the littlest bit of buy-in or participation. It gives people some ownership for success and gets their buy-in early on. That way, they're already part of the solution. The people you want to go to, of course, are the people other folks will follow—the people who carry a lot of weight in the informal power structure in your organization. If you can get even a small amount of buy-in from them, you can use it as leverage for sharing information.

Potential for Misinterpretation

New ideas are often met with skepticism. Don't be surprised if people think you're introducing your idea for selfish reasons, such as getting more authority or more power. One way to mitigate such reactions is to talk to people who are not familiar with your idea to see if they think there's any way it might be misinterpreted. Be direct. After explaining your idea and what you want to do with it, simply ask, "Do you think anyone could misinterpret my good intentions on this?" Depending on the answers you get, you can think about ways to prevent that misinterpretation. Above all, you want to present your idea as good for the organization, something that will help everybody in the long run.

Tips and Tactics

When you've scanned your organization and established where you can find some support and where you have to move carefully to avoid obstacles, you can start to work on actually communicating and implementing your idea. It's not surprising that many of these tactics fall under the umbrella of influencing others; after all, part of a leader's job is to gain commitment and alignment from others. Some of the tactics will draw on your skill at building and maintaining relationships, as well as your ability to create networks of support, to bolster your position with allies, and to create a reasoned and engaging argument for implementing your idea.

The more tactics you have to draw on, the more precise and effective action you can take in different situations. Rather than looking at this collection and asking which of them you can use, ask instead how you might use each of them. There may be some you can't use, but if you start by assuming that you can use all of them at one time or another, you can broaden your capacity for leading and your chances for success. Start by building as many options into your repertoire as you can so that when one tactic doesn't work or isn't available in a specific circumstance you can draw on another and keep moving forward.

Draw Attention to the Need or Opportunity

People will support your idea only when they realize that it is as important to them as it is to you. One way you can influence that view is to draw attention to the need, to make clear the nature of the problem. The kind of reaction you want to encourage is "I agree—that is a problem. How can we fix it?" You can then position your idea as the solution.

Another way to influence people is to draw attention to an opportunity. As with defining a problem, you must be really clear that there is room for improvement. A function in your organization may operate relatively well, but you can point to options and opportunities that will increase productivity or streamline operations enough to make implementing your idea worthwhile.

Needs and Opportunities

If people see something as a need, they see a problem that needs to be fixed. They recognize the problem, and you offer a solution—your idea. If people see something as an opportunity, it's a chance for improvement, and that may be a little harder to sell. People feel that things are already going well, and you're telling them that you want to improve something.

On the other hand, an improvement can be an easier sell in some ways. When you tell people that there's a need to fix something, you're implying that somebody has done something wrong and you're here to correct that. But if you say, "Things are going quite well, and I have an idea to make things even better, to build upon the successes we've already had," you're asking them to buy into an opportunity, and you're not implying that they've done anything wrong. The reception you get may be even better.

Create a Favorable Perception of Your Idea

When people hear that they should create a favorable perception, they often think that this means to put spin on the idea, to present it in a way that isn't fully authentic. But this isn't the case. An honest, positive presentation highlights the reasons you think your idea will work and why it's valuable. You should anticipate objections, and you should refine your idea so that it answers those objections.

Point out that you recognize that your idea isn't perfect. Every idea has flaws; none of us can anticipate every situation or

> You should anticipate objections, and you should refine your idea so that it answers those objections.

outcome. But in recognizing the flaws and in acknowledging objections, you can actually build support for your idea. You come across as looking for suggestions from others in overcoming those minor flaws that might detract from a very good idea. In this way you create joint ownership of the idea, which increases your base of support. It's great if the reaction to your idea is "That's a good idea, but I think there are some potential stumbling blocks. Did you ever think about doing it this way?" Then you've successfully made others part of your idea.

Leverage Past Support

Calling in favors sounds merely transactional: I scratched your back—now you scratch mine. But effectively selling your idea requires you to think more broadly than just quid pro quo. Think about the colleagues and peers that you've supported in the past. Was it because you had some resource they needed to successfully complete a project? If they had a resource gap and you were able to fill it, then you could look on this kind of mutual support as a means of balancing resources for the benefit of your organization rather than a simple trade.

Approach your request with a sense of negotiating a win-win scenario. Just as you aligned your resources with others in the past, now you are seeking to align their resources with your project. Assuming that your past efforts helped others accomplish their tasks, it's reasonable to assume that they will be open to helping you succeed as well, especially if you have done a good job of sharing information and promoting your idea as an opportunity or solution that needs the support of others to be realized.

Here's an approach you might use: "If you can help me get this project done, I think we can work together on another project that is more in line with what your group needs to accomplish. Together, we can do more than we can do on our own." Be open to options and suggestions, and keep encouraging a collaborative effort.

Start with Your Most Likely Allies

One common perception is that if you can sell an idea to your toughest audience, you can sell it to anyone. That view has some merit, but it's risky. You'll be more effective and have a better chance of success if you marshal your support early. Start with the people that you believe will be the most enthusiastic about your idea. This tactic does two good things: If you have difficulty selling the idea to your likely allies, you learn that your idea needs some work. If you sell your idea to people, they become allies, and you can use that group of allies as evidence that you're building consensus. People find it easier to support ideas that other people already support.

Start with the people that you believe will be the most enthusiastic about your idea.

Consider Possible Adjustments

Before you begin presenting your idea to others, think through some alternatives and adaptations you can make if you come up against resistance. What is your backup position? How far can you drop your expectations? It's important that you understand where your own line of compromise lies, where you can adapt without reducing your idea's potential effectiveness, and where you can't.

It's also important to consider your presentation so that you don't prompt an immediate negative response. People may react to your style of presentation before reacting to your idea, and you may lose any chance of getting their support.

Adjust your idea and your presentation proactively, not just in reaction to others. Seek feedback on both from your allies or from a trusted colleague who can serve as a sounding board and play devil's advocate.

Time It Right

Only you can decide when it's the best time to introduce your idea. Perhaps the groups in your organization are most open to new ideas at the end of a quarter, when they are making interme-

diate plans. If your organization has an annual strategy-making process, maybe you should time it for that cycle. Perhaps there is a time in the year when many people take vacation, and you can introduce your idea before they leave so that they can think about it. Or you can wait until they return, when they are refreshed and ready to tackle something new. Your timing depends much

upon the climate in your organization, whether it sets out plans at a specific time or is in a continual strategy-making mind-set. You need to determine how and when people are most willing to listen to new ideas—the situation can be different for every organization and for its groups.

You can increase your chances of success by aligning your idea with other events and ideas in your organization. This requires some research on your part. Find out what other groups are doing. Ask yourself whether your idea can increase their chances of success or benefit the outcome of their projects. On a larger

Leadership Task
Gather information about your organization's strategic goals and critical initiatives. Examine group and team plans throughout the organization and record their explicit goals. Speak to peers to see what their groups and teams are working on, what they want to achieve, and what their timelines are for completing their work. Examine this information and look for ways in which your idea can connect and what it has to offer in service of these different goals. Use what you've developed to help introduce and sell your idea as a piece of a larger initiative.

scale, familiarize yourself with your organization's strategy and its goals (short-term, intermediate, and long-term). If everyone in the organization is pursuing a specific goal, will your idea make it easier to achieve? If you attach your idea to current initiatives, which already enjoy organizational and individual support, you may find it easier to get endorsements and resources.

Use with Care

The following tactics can be very effective in selling your ideas to your organization, but if taken too far, they can be perceived as underhanded or sneaky. It's important to use them in an ethical way.

Work on a small scale to build momentum. You may be able to test your idea without introducing it fully into the organization.

A small-scale implementation will have a smaller impact on the organization if your idea doesn't work out as you'd planned. If you can test your idea with a few different parts of the organization, with a few different vendors, or with a few clients or customers, you can create a record of accomplishment that you can use to solicit broader support. Testing may also reveal flaws in your idea that you can correct and possible refinements that might make it more appealing to others.

Build in room to negotiate. Do you already know that your organization will cut 10 percent off anything and everything you request? If you know that you're going to have to negotiate, you may need to provide a high estimate of the amount of time and other resources you need. Then you can be talked down a little bit. What you don't want to do is to overstate your objectives or expectations. They have to be clear. If your organization is more straightforward and there's none of that artificial negotiation process, you won't need this tactic.

Explain the potential rewards and consequences. People tend to do what they get rewarded for. They may be thinking, or even saying, "What's in it for me?" You can explain the potential rewards—for individuals, groups, and the organization—of your getting buy-in for your idea and having it implemented. You can also explain the potential negative consequences at all different levels should your idea not be supported and not come to fruition.

Planning to Influence

Use this worksheet to plan ways to get improved buy-in for your idea.

Person/ Group to Influence	Why?	When?	Level of Support Needed	Why?	How to Influence This Person/Group

Closing the Deal

Selling an idea to a group or organization relies on two actions. First, you have to assess the environment into which you want to introduce your idea. Your group's way of doing things and your organization's climate will affect how people respond to your idea, to what degree they will support it, what kind and how many resources you are likely to gain for implementing your idea, and the chances of putting your idea into action.

Selling an idea to a group or organization relies on assessing the environment and using effective tactics.

Second are the tactical approaches you use to get your idea heard, supported, endorsed, and enacted. How you achieve each of these steps depends on your adapting your approach for different situations and for different constituencies in the organization. You can use the tactics described in this guidebook in various combinations, in different situations, and with different people inside and outside your organization.

A well-reasoned and engaging implementation plan is essential for making the most of any idea. But before the implementation comes the selling and the gathering of support. Assessing the environment in which your idea must thrive and considering how you can increase its chances of survival will prepare you for a successful campaign.

Suggested Readings

Baldwin, D., & Grayson, C. (2004). *Influence: Gaining commitment, getting results.* Greensboro, NC: Center for Creative Leadership.

Deal, T. E., & Kennedy, A. A. (2000). *Corporate cultures: The rites and rituals of corporate life.* New York: Basic Books.

Grayson, C., & Baldwin, D. (2007). *Leadership networking: Connect, collaborate, create.* Greensboro, NC: Center for Creative Leadership.

Heifetz, R. L., & Linsky, M. (2002). *Leadership on the line: Staying alive through the dangers of leading.* Boston: Harvard Business School Press.

Hernez-Broome, G., McLaughlin, C., & Trovas, S. (2006). *Selling yourself without selling out: A leader's guide to ethical self-promotion.* Greensboro, NC: Center for Creative Leadership.

Yukl, G. A. (2006). *Leadership in organizations* (6th ed.). Upper Saddle River, NJ: Prentice Hall.

Background

Many participants in CCL's educational programs discuss their need to learn how to better influence their organizations. They lament their inability to influence people over whom they have no direct authority. With the organizational structures emerging in our world today, this need to influence without authority is magnified.

Many of CCL's instruments have items that ask raters to assess a person's ability to influence them. In some CCL programs—The Looking Glass Experience and Foundations of Leadership, for example—participants receive direct feedback on their influencing skills. In Developing the Strategic Leader, the major focus is on thinking, acting, and influencing strategically.

Much of what this guidebook speaks to is the need to better understand and manage through organizational culture and politics. Participants often engage the facilitators in discussions about how to do this effectively, yet ethically. The increasingly global perspective and representation of the participants in our programs causes us to look at influencing from a variety of cultural viewpoints.

Key Point Summary

When you want to sell an idea to your organization, there are two important things to consider: an environmental scan and a collection of tactics.

Scanning your organizational environment lays the groundwork for success. You should assess how well your idea fits with your organization's goals, where you and your group are positioned in the true hierarchy of your organization, the level of support you need from key people in key groups, the kinds and amounts of resources you need, your own group's commitment to your idea, others who can help you sell or implement your idea, the possibility that others may feel threatened by your idea, and the possibility that your idea may be misinterpreted. Assessing these points will tell you what you know—and don't know.

When you've completed your scan of your organization, you can start to work on actually selling your idea. The following tactics can help: drawing attention to the need or opportunity, creating a favorable perception of your idea, leveraging past support, starting with your most likely allies, considering possible adjustments, and timing it right. You can also work on a small scale to build momentum, build in room to negotiate, and explain the potential rewards and consequences. The more tactics you have to draw on, the more precise and effective action you can take in different situations. Start by building as many options into your repertoire as you can so that when one tactic doesn't work or isn't available in a specific circumstance you can draw on another and keep moving forward.

Assessing the environment and considering tactics you can use will prepare you for a successful campaign. You will be more likely to accomplish your objective—solving the problem or making the improvement for the benefit of individuals, groups, and the organization as a whole.

Ordering Information

TO GET MORE INFORMATION, TO ORDER OTHER IDEAS INTO ACTION GUIDEBOOKS, OR TO FIND OUT ABOUT BULK-ORDER DISCOUNTS, PLEASE CONTACT US BY PHONE AT 336-545-2810 OR VISIT OUR ONLINE BOOKSTORE AT WWW.CCL.ORG/GUIDEBOOKS.

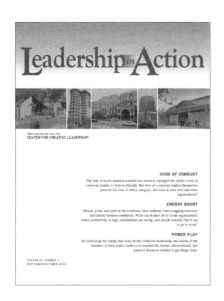

The articles in LiA give me insight into the various aspects of leadership and how they can be applied in my work setting.

Clayton H. Osborne
Vice President, Human Resources
Bausch & Lomb

LiA sparks ideas that help me better understand myself as a leader, both inside and outside the organization.

Kenneth Harris
Claims Director
Scottsdale Insurance Company

Leadership in Action

*A publication of the
Center for Creative Leadership
and Jossey-Bass/Wiley*

Leadership in Action is a bimonthly publication that aims to help practicing leaders and those who train and develop practicing leaders by providing them with insights gained in the course of CCL's educational and research activities. It also aims to provide a forum for the exchange of information and ideas between practitioners and CCL staff and associates.

To order, please contact Customer Service, Jossey-Bass, 989 Market Street, San Francisco, CA 94103-1741. Telephone: 888/378-2537; fax: 415/951-8553. See the Jossey-Bass Web site, at www.josseybass.com.